The Nation
Today's Mi

by Patricia Walsh

Scott Foresman
is an imprint of

Glenview, Illinois • Boston, Massachusetts • Chandler, Arizona
Upper Saddle River, New Jersey

Every effort has been made to secure permission and provide appropriate credit for photographic material. The publisher deeply regrets any omission and pledges to correct errors called to its attention in subsequent editions.

Unless otherwise acknowledged, all photographs are the property of Scott Foresman, a division of Pearson Education.

Photo locators denoted as follows: Top (T), Center (C), Bottom (B), Left (L), Right (R), Background (Bkgd)

Opener: (CL, CR) © Royalty-Free/Corbis, (B) ©DK Images; 1 (T) Getty Images, (C) Royalty-Free/Corbis; 3 (C) Getty Images, (B) Library of Congress; 4 (T) Getty Images, (BR) ©DK Images; 5 Library of Congress; 7 Getty Imagesl; 8 Library of Congress; 9 (BR) ©DK Images, (C) Getty Images, (T) Library of Congress; 10 (C) Getty Images, (CR) Library of Congress; 11 Library of Congress; 12 Library of Congress; 13 Library of Congress; 14 Library of Congress; 16 (CL, B) ©DK Images, (CR) Royalty-Free/Corbis; 17 (B) © Royalty-Free/Corbis; 18 Digital Wisdom, Inc.; 19 Getty Images; 20 ©DK Images; 23 Rubberball Productions

ISBN 13: 978-0-328-52152-4
ISBN 10:   0-328-52152-3

The Minutemen

In the early days of the American Revolution, much of the American army was a volunteer militia. The militia was made up of citizen-soldiers. These **citizen-soldiers** were regular people, mostly farmers. Each town had a militia that came together to defend the town from attack.

Some members of the Revolutionary militia gained the nickname "minutemen" because they could be ready to fight at a moment's notice. The minutemen were made famous in two poems about the American Revolution.

The various uniforms of the colonial troops

In the poem "Paul Revere's Ride" by Henry Wadsworth Longfellow, it is the minutemen who hear Paul Revere's warning as he rides into their towns on his horse, or **steed**. Revere's message is that the enemy British **troops** are coming to their towns. The militiamen are ready in a minute to stop the British.

In the hour of darkness and peril and need,
The people will waken and listen to hear
The hurrying hoof-beats of that steed,
And the midnight message of Paul Revere.

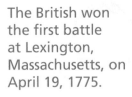

The British won the first battle at Lexington, Massachusetts, on April 19, 1775.

The minutemen were also made famous in these lines from the poem "Concord Hymn" by Ralph Waldo Emerson.

Here once the embattled farmers stood
And fired the shot heard round the world.

The "embattled farmers" in Emerson's poem are the minutemen. "The shot heard round the world" refers to the beginning of the American Revolution.

The United States still relies on citizen-soldiers. Today we call them the **National Guard.** Each state has U.S. Army and U.S. Air Force branches of the National Guard. Each Guard is under the command of its state governor. When public safety is threatened, the governor can order the state's National Guard to respond. If national security is threatened, the President can **mobilize,** or call up, any state's National Guard.

Early Militias

Early colonists found America to be a dangerous place. They felt the need to defend themselves from attack, so they created a **volunteer** militia. The oldest colonial volunteer group was the Ancient and Honorable Artillery Company. It began in Boston in 1638, long before the beginning of the American Revolution. When the American colonists were ready to declare themselves free from British rule in 1776, the colonial militias already had a long tradition of **defending** their towns and colonies. Those militias would play an important role in the American Revolution.

The thirteen English colonies along the Atlantic coast were prepared to defend themselves if necessary.

CLAIMED BY NEW HAMPSHIRE AND NEW YORK

MAINE (PART OF MASSACHUSETTS)

NEW HAMPSHIRE

MASSACHUSETTS

St. Lawrence River

Lake Huron

Lake Ontario

Lake Erie

NEW YORK

Hudson R.

Boston

RHODE ISLAND

CONNECTICUT

PENNSYLVANIA

New York City

NEW JERSEY

Philadelphia

Ohio River

DELAWARE

MARYLAND

VIRGINIA

N

NORTH CAROLINA

SOUTH CAROLINA

Savannah River

GEORGIA

Charleston

ATLANTIC OCEAN

40°N

65°W

35°N

30°N

St. Augustine (Spain)

Gulf of Mexico

25°N

	New England Colonies
	Middle Colonies
	Southern Colonies

0   250   500 Miles

0   250   500 Kilometers

70°W

Militias in the American Revolution

To gain their freedom from British rule, the colonists knew they would have to fight the British army. In 1774 the colonial leaders asked each colony to ready its militia. In Massachusetts, one-third of the militiamen prepared to instantly answer a call to battle. These were the first minutemen. Their first battle was in Lexington in 1775. Many of these volunteers later joined the new Continental Army to fight the British. The leader of this army was a former militia leader. His name was George Washington.

One American Revolutionary War hero, the Marquis de Lafayette, was from France. He came to America to help the colonists win their freedom from the British. When he returned to France, he fought in the French Revolution. He called his French troops the Garde Nationale. In honor of Lafayette and the help he gave during the American Revolution, New York State named its militia the National Guard.

Marquis de Lafayette

After the American Civil War (1861–1865), many states also renamed their militias. They too called their troops the National Guard. In 1916 the U.S. government passed a law that said all state militias would be renamed the National Guard.

Above: A U.S. Army recruiting poster

Below: A U.S. Army snare drum

The National Guard in War

Many of the most famous Civil War combat units were militia, not regular army units. One such unit was the Twentieth Maine, which helped win the Battle of Gettysburg.

In 1940, more than a year before the United States entered World War II, the National Guard was called up to serve the country. The National Guard was also mobilized for the Korean War in the 1950s. More recently, the Guard was called up for both the 1991 Persian Gulf War and the Iraq War.

Protecting Civil Rights

The National Guard has also been called to help where there is trouble at home. For a time in some places in the U.S., African American children were not allowed to attend the same schools as white children. In 1954 the U.S. Supreme Court ruled that all children have a right to an equal education and that African American children have the right to attend the same schools as white children.

In Tennessee some people disagreed with the Supreme Court's decision. The governor of Tennessee called up the National Guard to help him enforce the law that allowed integration, or the changing of the schools from all-white. The Guard protected the children as they walked past angry crowds to enter the new schools.

In Arkansas, the governor called up his state's National Guard to block African American students from attending the all-white schools. President Dwight D. Eisenhower had to order the Arkansas National Guard to enforce the law that said African American children had the right to attend those schools. The Guard followed the President's orders and protected the students as they began to attend classes in their new schools.

Left to right: the battlefield at Gettysburg, PA; Civil War soldiers; President Dwight Eisenhower

President John F. Kennedy

President John F. Kennedy called on the National Guard twice to protect the civil rights of citizens. In 1962 James Meredith, an African American, wanted to attend the all-white University of Mississippi. Many people at that time were still protesting the integration of public schools. President Kennedy called out more than ten thousand members of the National Guard. The Guard faced angry protestors and allowed the school to be integrated.

Then in 1963 Governor George Wallace of Alabama stood in the way of two African American students who wanted to enroll at the University of Alabama. But integration was the law, so President Kennedy ordered the Alabama National Guard to protect the students' rights. He wanted the Guard to make sure that all students could enroll at the university. Once again the Guard obeyed the President instead of the governor.

Governor George Wallace

The National Guard Called to Cities

In the summer of 1966, the tension over civil rights resulted in fighting in several cities across the country. The National Guard was called up to restore order. In Chicago, Illinois, the National Guard answered the call to protect the city. Four thousand Guard members, trained in **riot** control, were on the scene the same day that the governor called them up.

In Dayton, Ohio, one thousand members of the Guard were called out to stop the rioting. They rode along with policemen in police cars. They also patrolled the streets and guarded stores. The riots in Dayton ended three days later with the help from the Guard.

In San Francisco, California, more than three

thousand members of the Guard were called up to help stop a riot. Many members of the Guard had served during other California city riots and were trained for riot control. Using helmets and shields, the Guard controlled angry crowds and rapidly cleared the streets.

The following year in Milwaukee, Wisconsin, three thousand Guard members were called out to try to keep a riot from tearing apart the city. The Guard stopped all traffic to keep peace in the streets. Three days later, the Guard finally went home.

In the 1960s, people organized peaceful marches to protest inequality and the lack of civil rights for African Americans.

Training for the National Guard

Service in the National Guard begins with IET, or Initial Entry Training. In IET, the members of the Guard learn to live outdoors, to fight, and to stay safe. After IET, they usually train for one weekend each month and go to a two-week training period each year. The two-week training time is usually held in the summer. Many members of the Guard use their vacation time for summer training.

F-16 fighter jet

M1 Abrams tank

Providing Rescue and Relief

The National Guard is always ready for rescue and **relief** duty in emergencies and disasters. They help when natural disasters strike in the form of hurricanes, floods, tornadoes, heavy snowfalls, bitter cold, and drought.

During hurricanes, Guard members get through rising water in special trucks to evacuate stranded people. After tornadoes, the Guard cleans up fallen trees. At the height of blizzards, the Guard uses its big vehicles to rescue snowbound drivers and to clear roads. The National Guard is also ready to set up emergency generators to provide electricity when bad weather knocks down power lines. And Guard members give emergency medical help if people are hurt. They have even donated their own blood to help injured people.

The National Guard can help in other emergencies too. Its helicopters are used to drop water on forest fires or fly injured hikers out of the mountains. They are also used to search for missing skiers and snowboarders.

The National Guard in the World

The National Guard may be called upon to go to other countries around the world.

When the Iraqi army invaded its smaller neighbor Kuwait in August 1990, the National Guard was called up by President George H. W. Bush to go to Kuwait. More than sixty thousand Army National Guard men and women were called up. When the Gulf War began in January 1991, thousands of Guard members went overseas.

Protection of Citizens

The National Guard can move quickly when Americans are in need of protection. They direct traffic and control the crowds when the job is too big for local police. They also guard bridges, tunnels, and railroad and bus stations when extra protection is needed.

When asked, the National Guard patrols the nation's nuclear power plants and water reservoirs. They also have watched over the nation's airports.

The Guard protected the world's athletes during the 1996 Summer Olympics in Atlanta, Georgia, and the 2002 Winter Olympics in Salt Lake City, Utah.

Decisions to send the National Guard to countries all over the world are made at the U.S. Pentagon (below).

Women in the National Guard

At one time, the only women in the National Guard were nurses. This nurses-only rule was officially changed in 1967. The new rules allowed women to do many other military jobs too. The change in rules encouraged more women to join the Guard. Today there are more than thirty-five thousand women in the National Guard. Women perform many of the same functions as men, including combat roles. Like the men, they serve wherever they are needed.

1775 Minutemen at Lexington, MA	**1800**	**1861** American Civil War

The National Guard Museum

The National Guard Memorial Museum in Washington, D.C., tells people about the National Guard. It helps people understand why everyday citizens leave their jobs, families, and safety to serve in the National Guard. Visitors learn about the history of the Guard and its role in war and in peace.

Like the minutemen of years ago, the men and women of today's National Guard are quick to respond when called. They stand ready to become full-time soldiers if needed. They are ready to protect the people and property in each state. They are also ready to put aside their everyday lives to defend the United States at home and around the world.

A Historical Timeline: 1775 – 2003

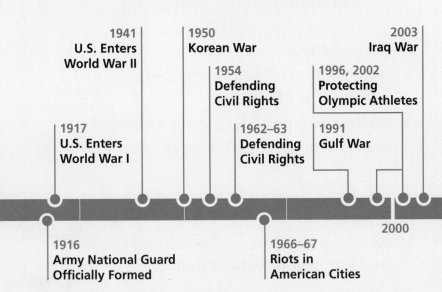

1941
U.S. Enters
World War II

1950
Korean War

2003
Iraq War

1954
Defending
Civil Rights

1996, 2002
Protecting
Olympic Athletes

1917
U.S. Enters
World War I

1962–63
Defending
Civil Rights

1991
Gulf War

2000

1916
Army National Guard
Officially Formed

1966–67
Riots in
American Cities

Now Try This

Call Up the National Guard!

Every state has a National Guard. It is under the command of the governor of the state. Each state has National Guard armories, or buildings where members of the Guard meet, train, and keep their equipment.

Find out about your state's National Guard, or choose another state to investigate. Use Internet or library resources to find the answers to the following questions.

- Decide which state's National Guard you are going to research.
- Who is the governor of the state?
- What is the population of the state?
- How many men and women currently serve in the state's National Guard?
- Where is the state's National Guard headquarters?
- How many National Guard armories are there in the state?
- What is one peacetime or wartime event in which this state's National Guard participated?
- How long do people serve in the National Guard?
- What are two jobs in the National Guard that a Guard member might do?

Now display your information in an easy-to-read format, such as a chart or a poster. Be sure to use a heading on your chart that tells which state's National Guard you are presenting. Draw a patch, or shoulder sleeve insignia, that someone serving in this state's National Guard might wear on his or her uniform. Attach your drawing to your chart or poster. Then share and compare your information with your classmates.

Glossary

citizen-soldiers *n.* people who are usually civilians but who can be called upon to be soldiers in times of peace or war.

defending *v.* protecting something or someone from harm.

mobilize *v.* call into active military service; organize for war.

National Guard *n.* trained military force of volunteer citizen-soldiers serving their state and nation.

relief *n.* aid; help.

riot *n.* a large group of people becoming noisy and out of control.

steed *n.* a high-spirited riding horse.

troops *n.* soldiers.

volunteer *adj.* formed or made up of volunteers, people who serve from their free will, not because they are forced to.